ESSENTIAL HEALING PRAYERS

ESSENTIAL HEALING PRAYERS

FOR PEACE AND STRENGTH

Written and compiled by
Mary Leonora Wilson, FSP

BOOKS & MEDIA

Boston

Nihil Obstat: Reverend James R. Mattaliano, S.J., M. Div., M.Th.
Imprimatur: ✠ Seán Cardinal O'Malley, O.F.M. Cap.
            Archbishop of Boston
            December 21, 2020

ISBN 10: 0-8198-2410-0
ISBN 13: 978-0-8198-2410-3

Published by Pauline Books & Media, 50 Saint Pauls Avenue, Boston, MA 02130-3491

Printed in the U.S.A.

www.pauline.org

Pauline Books & Media is the publishing house of the Daughters of Saint Paul, an international congregation of women religious serving the Church with the communications media.

1 2 3 4 5 6 7 8 9   25 24 23 22 21

Contents

Prayers to Mary,
Mother of Good Health

Prayers to the Angels
and the Saints

Prayers for a Good Death
and for the Dying

BASIC PRAYERS

Is anyone among you suffering? He should pray.
Is anyone in good spirits? He should sing praise. Is
anyone among you sick? He should summon the
presbyters of the church, and they should pray over
him and anoint him with oil in the name of the
Lord, and the prayer of faith will save the sick per-
son, and the Lord will raise him up. If he has com-
mitted any sins, he will be forgiven.

James 5:13–15

Introduction

Just to Touch His Cloak

The evangelists tell the story of a woman afflicted with hemorrhages for twelve years.[1] Reading the account, you can't help but feel the frustration of a woman who has tried everything: all the medical possibilities available to her, all the remedies offered in good advice, but everything to no avail. The evangelist Mark says that she only grew worse, left impoverished and in mental anguish. Due to her illness, she also found herself unaccepted in most circles of society. She has literally no options left—until Jesus enters her life.

She had heard about Jesus of Nazareth, whom many thought to be the Messiah. Hearing that he was in the village, faith was kindled in her heart; she began to hope again. So, quietly, but with determination, she "came up behind him in the crowd and touched his cloak. She said, 'If I but touch his clothes, I shall be cured.' Immediately her flow of blood dried up. She felt in her body that she was healed of her affliction. Jesus, aware at once that power had gone out from him, turned around in the crowd and asked, 'Who has touched my clothes?' But his disciples said to him, 'You see how the crowd is pressing upon you, and yet you ask, 'Who touched me?' And he looked around to see who had done it. The woman, realizing what had happened to her, approached, fearful and trembling. She fell down before Jesus and told him the whole truth. He said to her, 'Daughter, your faith has saved you. Go in peace and be cured of your affliction'" (Mk 5:27–34).

Most of us need healing on some level or another—healing of body, mind, or heart; of memories; of past or present wounds; of emotions, anxiety, fear; and of unhealthy or sinful habits. Jesus is the Divine Physician. He has the power to heal and the will to heal. A leper who approached him recognized this and said to him,

"If you will, you can make me clean." Jesus replied, "I do will it. Be made clean" (see Mt 8:3).

Faith does not exempt us from taking care of ourselves or of going to the doctor when necessary. On the contrary, it's part of the package. Living faith means being good stewards of all the gifts God has given us, and one of these is our health. However, there are times when the Lord lets us be visited by sickness for a greater good, or to draw us closer to him, to increase our faith and to experience his healing love and care. For some people, illness may actually be part of their vocation to holiness.

Prayers for healing are not some magical formulas for wellness. No. They are prayers that direct us to the loving providence of God and open us up to the healing action of the Holy Spirit. This may not always take the form that we expect it to, but as we pray and grow through suffering, we will feel the intervention of the Lord in our life and discover his healing love. May this be so for each of us.

Psalms for
Healing and Coping

The Psalms give voice to the perennial prayers of the people of God. The Psalter was the prayer book of the Jewish people and of Jesus; it remains the prayer book of the Church. Here we find prayers of petition and of praise, of thanksgiving and lament. Below you will find psalms that address the themes of illness, healing, and trust.

Psalm 6

Prayer for Recovery from Grave Illness

O Lord, do not rebuke me in your anger,
    or discipline me in your wrath.
Be gracious to me, O Lord, for I am
    languishing;

O Lord, heal me, for my bones are
    shaking with terror.
My soul also is struck with terror,
    while you, O Lord—how long?
Turn, O Lord, save my life;
    deliver me for the sake of your
        steadfast love.
For in death there is no remembrance
  of you;
    in Sheol who can give you praise?
I am weary with my moaning;
    every night I flood my bed with tears;
    I drench my couch with my weeping.
My eyes waste away because of grief;
    they grow weak because of all my foes.
Depart from me, all you workers of evil,
    for the Lord has heard the sound of
        my weeping.
The Lord has heard my supplication;
    the Lord accepts my prayer.
All my enemies shall be ashamed and struck
  with terror;
    they shall turn back, and in a moment
    be put to shame.

Psalm 23

The Divine Shepherd

The Lord is my shepherd, I shall not want.
    He makes me lie down in green
        pastures;
he leads me beside still waters;
    he restores my soul.
He leads me in right paths
    for his name's sake.
Even though I walk through the darkest
    valley,
    I fear no evil;
for you are with me;
    your rod and your staff—
    they comfort me.
You prepare a table before me
    in the presence of my enemies
you anoint my head with oil;
    my cup overflows.
Surely goodness and mercy shall follow me
    all the days of my life,
and I shall dwell in the house of the Lord
    my whole life long.

Psalm 27

Prayer of Confidence

The Lord is my light and my salvation;
     whom shall I fear?
The Lord is the stronghold of my life;
     of whom shall I be afraid?
When evildoers assail me
     to devour my flesh—
my adversaries and foes—
     they shall stumble and fall.
Though an army encamp against me,
     my heart shall not fear;
though war rise up against me,
     yet I will be confident.
One thing I asked of the Lord,
     that will I seek after:
to live in the house of the Lord
     all the days of my life,
to behold the beauty of the Lord,
     and to inquire in his temple.
For he will hide me in his shelter
     in the day of trouble;

he will conceal me under the cover of
    his tent;
        he will set me high on a rock.
Now my head is lifted up
    above my enemies all around me,
and I will offer in his tent
    sacrifices with shouts of joy;
I will sing and make melody to the Lord.
Hear, O Lord, when I cry aloud,
    be gracious to me and answer me!
"Come," my heart says, "seek his face!"
    Your face, Lord, do I seek.
    Do not hide your face from me.
Do not turn your servant away in anger,
    you who have been my help.
Do not cast me off, do not forsake me,
    O God of my salvation!
If my father and mother forsake me,
    the Lord will take me up.
Teach me your way, O Lord,
    and lead me on a level path
    because of my enemies.
Do not give me up to the will of my
    adversaries,

for false witnesses have risen against me,
and they are breathing out violence.
I believe that I shall see the goodness of the
Lord
in the land of the living.
Wait for the Lord;
be strong, and let your heart take courage;
wait for the Lord!

Psalm 38

A Penitent Sufferer's Plea for Healing

O Lord, do not rebuke me in your anger,
or discipline me in your wrath.
For your arrows have sunk into me,
and your hand has come down on me.
There is no soundness in my flesh
because of your indignation;
there is no health in my bones
because of my sin.
For my iniquities have gone over my head;
they weigh like a burden too heavy for
me.
My wounds grow foul and fester

because of my foolishness;
I am utterly bowed down and prostrate;
    all day long I go around mourning.
For my loins are filled with burning,
    and there is no soundness in my flesh.
I am utterly spent and crushed;
    I groan because of the tumult of my
        heart.
O Lord, all my longing is known to you;
    my sighing is not hidden from you.
My heart throbs, my strength fails me;
    as for the light of my eyes—it also has
        gone from me.
My friends and companions stand aloof
  from my affliction,
    and my neighbors stand far off.
Those who seek my life lay their snares;
    those who seek to hurt me speak of
        ruin,
    and meditate treachery all day long.
But I am like the deaf, I do not hear;
    like the mute, who cannot speak.
Truly, I am like one who does not hear,
    and in whose mouth is no retort.

But it is for you, O Lord, that I wait;
  it is you, O Lord my God, who will
    answer.
For I pray, "Only do not let them rejoice
  over me,
    those who boast against me when my
      foot slips."
For I am ready to fall,
  and my pain is ever with me.
I confess my iniquity;
  I am sorry for my sin.
Those who are my foes without cause are
  mighty,
    and many are those who hate me
      wrongfully.
Those who render me evil for good
  are my adversaries because I follow
    after good.
Do not forsake me, O Lord;
  O my God, do not be far from me;
make haste to help me,
  O Lord, my salvation.

Psalm 41

Assurance of God's Help and a Plea for Healing

Happy are those who consider the poor;
    the Lord delivers them in the day
        of trouble.
The Lord protects them and keeps them
    alive;
        they are called happy in the land.
        You do not give them up to the will of
            their enemies.
The Lord sustains them on their sickbed;
        in their illness you heal all their
            infirmities.
As for me, I said, "O Lord, be gracious
    to me;
        heal me, for I have sinned against you."
My enemies wonder in malice
    when I will die, and my name perish.
And when they come to see me, they utter
    empty words,
        while their hearts gather mischief;
        when they go out, they tell it abroad.

All who hate me whisper together about me;
    they imagine the worst for me.
They think that a deadly thing has fastened
    on me,
        that I will not rise again from where I
            lie.
Even my bosom friend in whom I trusted,
    who ate of my bread, has lifted the
        heel against me.
But you, O Lord, be gracious to me,
    and raise me up, that I may repay them.
By this I know that you are pleased with me;
    because my enemy has not triumphed
        over me.
But you have upheld me because of my
    integrity,
    and set me in your presence forever.
Blessed be the Lord, the God of Israel,
    from everlasting to everlasting.
Amen and Amen.

Psalm 56

Trust in God

Be gracious to me, O God, for people
   trample on me;
      all day long foes oppress me;
my enemies trample on me all day long,
   for many fight against me.
O Most High, when I am afraid,
   I put my trust in you.
In God, whose word I praise,
   in God I trust; I am not afraid;
   what can flesh do to me?
All day long they seek to injure my cause;
   all their thoughts are against me for
      evil.
They stir up strife, they lurk,
   they watch my steps.
As they hoped to have my life,
   so repay them for their crime;
   in wrath cast down the peoples, O God!
You have kept count of my tossings;
   put my tears in your bottle.
   Are they not in your record?

Then my enemies will retreat
  in the day when I call.
  This I know, that God is for me.
In God, whose word I praise,
  in the Lord, whose word I praise,
in God I trust; I am not afraid.
  What can a mere mortal do to me?
My vows to you I must perform, O God;
  I will render thank offerings to you.
For you have delivered my soul from death,
  and my feet from falling,
so that I may walk before God
  in the light of life.

Psalm 62

Waiting for the Lord

For God alone my soul waits in silence;
  from him comes my salvation.
He alone is my rock and my salvation,
  my fortress; I shall never be shaken.
How long will you assail a person,
  will you batter your victim, all of you,
  as you would a leaning wall, a tottering
    fence?

Their only plan is to bring down a person
     of prominence.
          They take pleasure in falsehood;
they bless with their mouths,
          but inwardly they curse.
For God alone my soul waits in silence,
          for my hope is from him.
He alone is my rock and my salvation,
          my fortress; I shall not be shaken.
On God rests my deliverance and my honor;
          my mighty rock, my refuge is in God.
Trust in him at all times, O people;
          pour out your heart before him;
          God is a refuge for us.
Those of low estate are but a breath,
          those of high estate are a delusion;
in the balances they go up;
          they are together lighter than a breath.
Put no confidence in extortion,
          and set no vain hopes on robbery;
          if riches increase, do not set your heart
               on them.
Once God has spoken;
          twice have I heard this:

that power belongs to God,
   and steadfast love belongs to you,
      O Lord.
For you repay to all
   according to their work.

Psalm 70

Prayer for Deliverance

Be pleased, O God, to deliver me.
   O Lord, make haste to help me!
Let those be put to shame and confusion
   who seek my life.
Let those be turned back and brought
   to dishonor
      who desire to hurt me.
Let those who say, "Aha, Aha!"
   turn back because of their shame.
Let all who seek you
   rejoice and be glad in you.
Let those who love your salvation
   say evermore, "God is great!"
But I am poor and needy;
   hasten to me, O God!

You are my help and my deliverer;
O Lord, do not delay!

Psalm 88

Prayer for Help in Despondency

O Lord, God of my salvation,
when, at night, I cry out in your
presence,
let my prayer come before you;
incline your ear to my cry.
For my soul is full of troubles,
and my life draws near to Sheol.
I am counted among those who go down
to the Pit;
I am like those who have no help,
like those forsaken among the dead,
like the slain that lie in the grave,
like those whom you remember no more,
for they are cut off from your hand.
You have put me in the depths of the Pit,
in the regions dark and deep.
Your wrath lies heavy upon me,
and you overwhelm me with all your
waves.

You have caused my companions to shun me;
    you have made me a thing of horror to
        them.
I am shut in so that I cannot escape;
    my eye grows dim through sorrow.
Every day I call on you, O Lord;
    I spread out my hands to you.
Do you work wonders for the dead?
    Do the shades rise up to praise you?
Is your steadfast love declared in the grave,
    or your faithfulness in Abaddon?
Are your wonders known in the darkness,
    or your saving help in the land of
        forgetfulness?
But I, O Lord, cry out to you;
    in the morning my prayer comes
        before you.
O Lord, why do you cast me off?
    Why do you hide your face from me?
Wretched and close to death from my
    youth up,
    I suffer your terrors; I am desperate.
Your wrath has swept over me;
    your dread assaults destroy me.

They surround me like a flood all day long;
 	from all sides they close in on me.
You have caused friend and neighbor to
 	shun me;
 	my companions are in darkness.

Psalm 146

Praise for God's Help

Praise the Lord!
Praise the Lord, O my soul!
I will praise the Lord as long as I live;
 	I will sing praises to my God all my
 	 	life long.
Do not put your trust in princes,
 	in mortals, in whom there is no help.
When their breath departs, they return to
 	the earth;
 	on that very day their plans perish.
Happy are those whose help is the God of
 	Jacob,
 	whose hope is in the Lord their God,
who made heaven and earth,
 	the sea, and all that is in them;

who keeps faith forever;
>who executes justice for the oppressed;
who gives food to the hungry.
The Lord sets the prisoners free;
>the Lord opens the eyes of the blind.
The Lord lifts up those who are bowed
down;
>the Lord loves the righteous.
The Lord watches over the strangers;
>he upholds the orphan and the widow,
>but the way of the wicked he brings to
>ruin.
The Lord will reign forever,
>your God, O Zion, for all generations.
Praise the Lord!

More psalms of healing and coping for your prayer: 4, 13, 16, 22, 31, 34, 40, 57, 71, 86, 90, 91, 102, 103, 107, 116, 138.

Prayers to God:
Father, Son, and Holy Spirit

Prayers of Intercession

Prayer for the Sick

All-powerful God, salvation for all those who believe and hope in you, because your own Son experienced immense pain and suffering during his passion, we can feel assured that you understand our suffering and grief. Listen to my prayer for (*name*) and for all the sick, the distressed, and those oppressed by pain.

Grant them strength in weakness and grace to believe in your presence with us: "It is I; do not be afraid" (Jn 6:20). Accompanied by this strength of your consolation, may we learn from Jesus the transforming power of suffering and trust in your never-failing love. Through your Son, our Lord Jesus Christ, in the unity of the Holy Spirit, one God forever and ever. Amen.

Prayer During a Pandemic

Loving Father, in these days of widespread illness and anxiety, we turn to you in trust. You desire all that is good for us: our physical and spiritual well-being, our health and wholeness. We ask you to free us from all deadly viruses and from all serious illnesses and to protect us from the even more pervasive virus of sin.

Have mercy on us and especially on all who have died.

Jesus, Divine Physician, many of those you love are sick; bring healing to those in the grip of illness. Safeguard and bless doctors, nurses, caregivers, pastoral ministers, volunteers, and first responders. Grant peace to the anxious and be near those who are concerned for sick family members and loved ones. Comfort those who mourn and let their grief be lightened by their hope in the eternal life you won for us, where every tear is washed away and there is no more suffering or death.

All-powerful, Holy Spirit, enlighten those men and women producing a vaccine to combat this virus. Inspire government and civil leaders as they strive to contain the disease, and let everyone collaborate to make their work easier and successful.

Merciful and Triune-God, may social distancing teach us to be more creative in showing compassion and in reaching out to one another in solidarity and love. Preserve the elderly, the underprivileged, and the most vulnerable from loneliness, discouragement and mental anguish. Sustain those who have suffered financial loss or unemployment. Unite us with one another and with you in hope and love. Do not let fear prevail.

Mary our Mother and Health of the Sick, we take refuge under your protective mantle. Intercede for us with your Divine Son as you did at Cana, that he may transform our anxiety into trust, illness into health, death into life. Teach us to learn from this how to live in ever greater communion with the Lord and with each other, appreciative of the gifts we have received, generous in sharing, overflowing with gratitude. Amen.

Prayer for a Loved One Suffering Depression[2]

My Father and my God, I turn to you in quiet confidence. I pray by the power of your Holy Spirit that you lift my loved one from the abyss of deepening depression. Return to him/her the colors of your joy! Father, at creation you separated the light from darkness. I ask you to create that light within his/her life once more. Give unto him/her eyes that see with your Spirit that all is well with you. Let the shadows that now enfold him/her be cast away by the power of the cross of my Lord and Savior Jesus. May Jesus intercede where he/she cannot. I ask this because of your love and faithfulness. Amen.

Prayer for the Needs of Others

God of love, whose compassion never fails,
we bring you the sufferings of the world:
the needs of the homeless,
the cries of prisoners,
the pains of the sick and injured,

the sorrow of the bereaved,
the helplessness of the elderly and weak.
to their needs and your great mercy,
strengthen and relieve them in Jesus Christ
   our Lord.

Saint Anselm

Prayer for Those Who Are Terminally Ill

Lord Jesus, you healed so many people during your public ministry. I bring before you now, in prayer, all those who are terminally ill and have no hope of recovery.

Look lovingly and compassionately upon them. Let them feel the strength of your consolation. Help them and their families to accept this cross they are asked to carry.

Let them experience your presence as you carry their cross with them. May Mary be there too, to comfort them.

Lord Jesus, I know and believe that, if it is your will, you can cure those I pray for especially (*name*). I place my trust in you. I pray with faith, but I also pray as you did in Gethsemane: your will be done.

Bless us, Lord, and hear my prayer. Amen.

Let Them Know We Care[3]

As I watch the struggle, feeling helpless,
as I watch her/him feeling alone,
both of us knowing there is nothing I can
    do to end the pain,
Lord, help her/him to get through the day.
Help to make each day better than the
    day before.
Let her/him know that we care, and that
    she/he is not alone.
Help her/him to understand that she/he
    will get by.
Watch over those who may have lost hope,
or may at some time reach that point.
Help them to feel not only your uncondi-
    tional love,
but the love of those around them.
Let them know we care now and always will.

Prayer for Abused Children

Heavenly Father, Jesus assured us that you have a special care for children. You have given each one of them an angel to protect them from harm and guide them along life's ways.

Please hear our prayers for the thousands of abused children in the world and in our country. This is one of the saddest evils of our day, one that cries to you for justice. We beg you to convert those who ruin the innocence of children, those who betray their trust, those who exploit them for selfish and depraved purposes, and those who physically injure and kill them.

Remember the childhood of your Son, Jesus; you sent an angel to rescue him from harm's way. Bless and protect all these innocent lives that are so dear to you. Rescue those children who are in unsafe homes and environments; protect them from people of evil intent. Provide them with parents, teachers, friends, caregivers, who will love and protect them. Be their shield, their comforter, their safety. And may we, most merciful Father, in our families, parishes, schools, and communities do all we can for the welfare and protection of children and the formation of adults, creating a better world for all of us.

Help those who have been abused to find help, healing, and true love so that they can become strong and confident. Bind up their wounds, heal their hearts, restore their betrayed and broken trust. Let them experience that they have a Father in heaven who loves them.

Dearest Mother Mary, gather these most vulnerable of your children under your mantle and surround them with your motherly love.

We ask this all in the name of Jesus, who shared our weakness in all things but sin, and lives and reigns with you, Father, in the unity of the Holy Spirit forever and ever. Amen.

Prayer for Those Who Have Left Home

Jesus, Good Shepherd, there are still many wandering sheep in the world today. There are many grieving relatives and friends who do not know where their loved ones have gone.

Pour your healing love both on those who grieve and those who have left home. Seek them out and touch their wounds—whatever may have caused them to leave home.

Remind them of the prodigal son and the lost sheep. Make both sides willing to forgive and reconcile—to start life over, a new life of greater care and concern.

Guardian angels protect from dangers your runaway charges, and never abandon them. May you lead them home again to a beautiful family reunion. Amen.

Prayer for Healing for Victims of Abuse

Merciful Father, protector of all who hope in you, strength of the weak, and guardian of the defenseless, hear the cries of our brothers and sisters whose trust has been betrayed and who have been gravely harmed in body, mind and spirit. Heal their wounds; release them from bitterness and shame; renew them in your love and help them trust in your Son's victory over evil. May Jesus transform their brokenness into wholeness.

Grant that all those who have been abused find among us understanding and support, respect and compassion. Strengthen them with the gifts of your Divine Spirit, letting them find peace in a just atonement and in surrender to your healing mercy.

We ask this through Christ, our Lord. Amen.

The Chaplet of Divine Mercy

(This may be prayed using a five-decade rosary.)

> The soul that trusts in My mercy is most fortunate, because I Myself take care of it.
>
> *Jesus to Saint Faustina Kowalska, Diary, 1273*

Jesus himself dictated the Chaplet of Divine Mercy to Saint Faustina Kowalska. In this prayer we offer Jesus—Body, Blood, Soul and Divinity—to God the Father, and we unite ourselves with his sacrifice offered on the Cross for the salvation of the world. We hand over all our needs and ask for mercy for ourselves and for all people: those living on earth and the souls in purgatory.

Begin with an Our Father, Hail Mary, and Apostles' Creed.

On the single bead before each decade:

Eternal Father, I offer you the Body and Blood, Soul and Divinity of your dearly beloved Son, our Lord Jesus Christ, in atonement for our sins and those of the whole world.

On the ten beads of each decade:

For the sake of his sorrowful passion, have mercy on us and on the whole world.

After the five decades, conclude with:

Holy God, Holy Mighty One, Holy Immortal One, have mercy on us and on the whole world (*3 times*).

Saint Faustina Kowalska

Personal Prayers

Invocations of Trust from Saint Faustina's Diary

O my God, my only hope, I have placed all my trust in you, and I know I shall not be disappointed (317).

I know the full power of your mercy, and I trust that you will give me everything your weak child needs (898).

O Jesus, concealed in the Blessed Sacrament of the altar, my only love and mercy, I commend to you all the needs of my body and soul. You can help me because you are mercy itself. In you lies all my hope (1751).

In Times of Anxiety

Father, I know that your love never fails and that you care for everything you have made. Whatever the troubles of our hearts, you guide and sustain us. May the beauty of your creation—the lilies of the field and the birds of the air (see Lk 12:24 and 27)—be a constant reminder to me that nothing you have made is ever forgotten.

In moments of fear, give me courage; when I am overwhelmed by anxiety, give me renewed faith in your loving providence. I ask this through Jesus, your Son. Amen.

A Prayer When Feeling Depressed

God, our Father, your Son Jesus expressed his feelings of desolation when he prayed to you from the cross. Help me to believe in your great goodness and love, even though I cannot always feel them, teach me to value this time of darkness and await the rediscovery of your abiding presence and tender concern. Grant me the grace to remain constant in hope, despite the darkness that seems to hide it from me, and to be confident that you walk with me even here. Strengthen my conviction that although I am journeying through this dark night now, I will one day enjoy the never-ending light of eternal life. I ask you this through Jesus Christ, my Lord and Redeemer. Amen.

A Prayer of Self-Care

Lord God, you have called me into life, formed me in your image and likeness, and made me your holy temple. You have given me a body to serve you and others, a mind to know things and reflect on them, a heart to love you and all people. Help me to care for these wonderful gifts and to use them wisely for your glory, my own growth, and the good of others. Bless me with your grace, O Lord, and with the strength I need for each day. Help me to keep boundaries, while living compassionately and generously, to respect my limitations and those of others. Give me patience with myself and with those around me, a sense of humor and the ability to laugh at myself, a peaceful spirit, and a forgiving heart. Help me to live this day in your presence, knowing you are with me always, the source of my joy and my strength. Amen.

Prayer to Jesus, the Divine Physician

Lord Jesus, you are the Divine Physician, Healer of body and soul, mind and spirit. Please grant me good health, so that I may glorify you in serving others and proclaiming the good news of your Gospel. Guard and protect me from serious illness and from every danger to body and soul.

Father, free my mind from all anxiety and fear, from all judgmental, proud, and discouraging thoughts, and let me put on the mind of your beloved Son, Jesus Christ.

Holy Spirit, Spirit of Life and of Love, let my heart be rooted in Christ and built on him; let his love and his peace reign in me so that I may radiate that same peace and goodness to others in need. Preserve me, mind and body, as a holy temple of your presence.

Blessed Trinity, may I be mindful of your presence always. Fill me with a spirit of thankfulness and joy, so that my life may be a living offering of praise to you.

Watch over me as I work and play, as I rest and sleep, protecting me—mind, soul and body. May my life glorify you today and every day. Amen.

In Times of Illness

Jesus, Divine Physician, you responded to the needs of the sick with compassion and a generous heart. Be with me in my illness and stay by my side. Let me not lose sight of you or doubt your presence.

Grant me great faith and trust in your mercy. Help me to experience your healing power in my mind, heart, body, and soul. I unite myself in this suffering to your cross, so my illness can bring spiritual benefit to me and to others.

May bearing the cross of sickness here on earth help to purify and prepare me for an eternity of perfect joy and happiness in the fullness of life with you and the Father and Holy Spirit forever in Heaven. Amen.

Prayer of a Person with a Terminal Illness

Heavenly Father, Abba, I am broken in spirit and body by this illness that I have been told is very serious and will probably lead to my death.

Instinctively I ask, "Why, Lord? Show me what I did wrong. Why are you angry with me? How can you let this happen to me?"

I have heard that those who have the heaviest crosses are those you love most. It is very hard for me to believe that right now, so please help me. Let the ray of your miraculous love pierce the darkness that is flooding my soul.

Once I know you love me, I can bear anything with joy, because I will possess the only thing that can really make me happy.

Please touch my family and friends also, so that together we can enjoy your consolation during this difficult situation. Amen.

Prayer for Inner Healing[4]

Lord Jesus, you came to heal
our wounded and troubled hearts.
I beg you to heal the torments that
cause anxiety in my heart;
I beg you in particular to heal
all those that are a cause of sin.
I beg you to come into my life

and heal me of the psychological harms
that struck me in my early years,
and from the injuries that it caused
throughout my life.
Lord Jesus, you know my burdens.
I lay them all on your Good Shepherd's Heart.
I beseech you—by the merits of the great,
    open wound in your heart—
to heal the small wounds that are in mine.
Heal the pain of my memories,
so that nothing that has happened to me
will cause me to remain in pain and anguish,
filled with anxiety.
Heal, O Lord,
all those wounds that have been
the cause of all the evil that is rooted in
    my life.
I want to forgive
all those who have offended me.
Look to those inner sores
that make me unable to forgive.
You who came to forgive the afflicted
    of heart,

please, heal my own heart.
Heal, my Lord Jesus, those intimate wounds
that cause me physical illness.
I offer you my heart.
Accept it, Lord, purify it, and give me
the sentiments of your Divine Heart. . . .
Make me an authentic witness
to your resurrection,
your victory over sin and death,
your living presence among us.

Healing from Sexual Abuse[5]

Lord, you called me into being and made me good. You graced me with your life in Baptism. Because of this, I can trust that you love me with the tenderness of a mother and the strength of a loving father. Yet things have been done to me that cause me to feel ashamed, unclean, and unworthy. Heal my memory of the wounds of abuse. Restore my self-esteem and heal my fear of intimacy and trust. Help me to build good relationships with others. Keep reminding me that you made all of me good: body and soul.

Forgive those who harmed and violated me. Heal them of their disorders. May I never harm others in any way. Grant me courage to begin anew in peace, serenity, confidence, and grace. Amen.

Prayer for the Healing of Memories

Loving Father, I come before you with faith, trusting in your unconditional and constant love for me. Jesus has promised that whatever we ask for in his name we will receive, provided it be according to your holy will and for the good of my soul. I come to you believing in that promise.

I come as I am, in all my woundedness and visited by painful memories that still surface in my heart and mind and cause so much anguish and distress. You know how much I suffer because of these memories.

I beg you, enter my heart and heal all my wounded emotions. Bring your healing love into every corner of my being. Release all the buried negative memories and unhealed hurts that block the flow of your grace, robbing me of your peace, love, and joy. Help me to accept them as part of my salvation history and your redeeming love.

Remove every feeling of sadness, loneliness, fear, and anxiety. Wash away all guilt, despair, feelings of betrayal and rejection. Heal all feelings of anger, hatred, resentment, and bitterness.

Pour out your Spirit of healing on all the memories and emotions that cause feelings of hopelessness, discouragement, helplessness, shame, and despair. Grant me the grace to forgive all who have hurt me and likewise to be forgiven by those whom I have harmed.

And then, dear Father, after I have been healed, make me a joyful witness of your healing power, that I may bring glory, honor, and praise to you.

I ask everything in Jesus' name. Amen.

Litany of Trust[6]

From the belief that I have to earn your love,
  Response: deliver me, Jesus.

From the fear that I am unlovable, *R.*

From the false security that I have what
  it takes, *R.*

From the fear that trusting you will leave
  me more destitute, *R.*

From all suspicion of your words and
  promises, *R.*

From the rebellion against childlike
  dependency on you, *R.*

From refusals and reluctances in accepting
  your will, *R.*

From anxiety about the future, *R.*

From resentment or excessive preoccupation
  with the past, *R.*

From restless self-seeking in the present
  moment, *R.*

From disbelief in your love and presence, *R.*

From the fear of being asked to give more
  than I have, *R.*

From the belief that my life has no meaning
   or worth, *R.*

From the fear of what love demands, *R.*

From discouragement, *R.*

   Response: *Jesus, I trust in you.*

That you are continually holding me,
   sustaining me, loving me, *R.*

That your love goes deeper than my sins
   and failings, and transforms me, *R.*

That not knowing what tomorrow brings
   is an invitation to lean on you, *R.*

That you are with me in my suffering,

That my suffering, united to your own,
   will bear fruit in this life and the next, *R.*

That you will not leave me an orphan, *R.*

That you are present in your Church, *R.*

That your plan is better than anything else, *R.*

That you always hear me and in your goodness always respond to me, *R.*

That you give me the grace to accept
   forgiveness and to forgive others, *R.*

That you give me all the strength I need
    for what is asked, *R.*

That my life is a gift, *R.*

That you will teach me to trust you, *R.*

That you are my Lord and my God, *R.*

That I am your beloved one. Amen.

Unfailing Prayer for Hope

Lord Jesus, you see my entire life.
You know my thoughts and feelings.
You see how hard life can be,
how unfair it can seem at times.
In all the confusion, one thing is certain:
your love for me never changes.
I place all my hope in you.
Embrace me as I am.
Walk with me and guide me.
Let me follow where you lead.
You desire only the greatest good for me;
you are on my side.
I place all my hope in you.
Help me see how much

you want to be part of my life.
Teach me to follow you in trust.
You are God, my Savior.
I place all my hope in you.
Blessing: "May the God of hope fill me
with all joy and peace in believing,
so that I might abound in hope by
the power of the Holy Spirit" (see Rom
15:13).

Prayer before Surgery[7]

Lord, I have faith that you will be with me
    during my surgery.
Lord, I have hope that you will guide those
    entrusted with my surgery.
Lord, while I do not love the idea of
    this surgery, I do love you.
Thus, I praise you and give you thanks
    for this opportunity . . .
my praise and thanksgiving to be
        continued.

Prayer after Surgery[8]

Praise the Lord! It's over!
I'm a little uncomfortable now,
but I did not forget my promise to return
with thankfulness and praise.
I knew you were there—you never forget any
    of those you love.
Thank you for the doctors and nurses who
    performed my operation,
for family and friends who prayed for its
    success,
and for those who attended me in recovery.
Dear Lord, keep me mindful of all those who
    undergo surgical procedures.
Bless them and protect them as you have
    blessed and protected me. Amen.

Healing Prayer by Padre Pio

Heavenly Father, I thank you for loving me. I
thank you for sending your Son, Our Lord Jesus
Christ, to the world to save and to set me free. I
trust in your power and grace that sustain and

restore me. Loving Father, touch me now with your healing hands, for I believe that your will is for me to be well in mind, body, soul, and spirit.

Cover me with the most precious blood of your Son, our Lord Jesus Christ from the top of my head to the soles of my feet. Cast out anything that should not be in me. Root out any unhealthy and abnormal cells. Open any blocked arteries or veins, and rebuild and replenish any damaged areas. Remove all inflammation and cleanse any infection by the power of Jesus' precious blood. Let the fire of your healing love pass through my entire body to heal and make new any diseased areas so that my body will function the way you created it to function. Touch also my mind and my emotion, even the deepest recesses of my heart.

Saturate my entire being with your presence, love, joy, and peace and draw me ever closer to you every moment of my life. And Father, fill me with your Holy Spirit and empower me to do your works so that my life will bring glory and honor to your holy name. I ask this in the name of the Lord Jesus Christ. Amen.

Help Me to Have Perfect Trust

O Christ Jesus, when all is darkness and I feel my weakness and helplessness, give me a sense of your presence, your love, and your strength. Help me to have perfect trust in your protecting love and strengthening power, so that nothing may frighten or worry me, for, living close to you, I shall see your hand, your purpose, your will through all things. Amen.

Saint Ignatius of Loyola

To Obtain Good Health

O Divine Holy Spirit, Creator and Renewer of all things, Life of my life, with Mary most holy I adore you, I thank you, I love you!

You give life and vivify the whole universe. Preserve me in good health; free me from the illnesses which threaten it and all the evils which endanger it.

Assisted by your grace, I promise to always use my energies for the glory of God, for the good of my soul, and in the service of my brothers and sisters.

I pray too that you illumine with your gifts of knowledge and understanding all doctors and those who care for the sick, so that they may know the true causes of the ills which endanger and threaten life and may discover and apply the most effective remedies to defend life and heal it.

Virgin Most Holy, Mother of life and Health of the sick, to you I entrust this humble prayer of mine. Mother of God, and our Mother, deign to increase its value with your powerful intercession. Amen.

Blessed James Alberione

Heal Me, Holy Spirit

Holy Spirit, through the intercession of the Queen of Pentecost:

Heal my mind of lack of reflection, of ignorance, forgetfulness, obstinacy, prejudice, error, and perversion, and form Jesus Christ-Truth in everything.

Heal my heart of indifference, diffidence, bad inclinations, passions, overly sentimental feelings, and attachments, and form Jesus Christ-Life in everything.

Heal my will of lack of willpower, fickleness, inconstancy, sloth, stubbornness, and bad habits, and form Jesus Christ-Way in me.

Give me a new love for whatever Jesus loves and for Jesus himself.

Let there be a new Pentecost and let me be a new apostle, gifted with the spirit of wisdom, knowledge, understanding, counsel, piety, fortitude, and holy fear of God.

Blessed James Alberione

In Every Need

Holy Spirit,
my light, my love, my strength,
be with me now and always.
In all my doubts, anxieties, and trials,
   come, Holy Spirit.
In hours of loneliness, weariness, and grief,
   come, Holy Spirit.
In failure, in loss, and in disappointment,
   come, Holy Spirit.

When others fail me, when I fail myself,
   come, Holy Spirit.
When I am ill, unable to work, depressed,
   come, Holy Spirit.
Now and forever, and in all things,
   come, Holy Spirit.

Prayers to Mary,
Mother of Good Health

The Memorare

Remember, O most gracious Virgin Mary,
that never was it known
that anyone who fled to your protection,
implored your help, or sought your
    intercession was left unaided.
Inspired with this confidence, I fly to you,
    O virgins of virgins, my Mother.
To you I come, before you I stand, sinful
    and sorrowful.
O Mother of the Word Incarnate,
despise not my petitions, but in your
    mercy, hear and answer me. Amen.

O Mary, My Queen

O Mary, my Queen, I cast myself into the
arms of your mercy.

I place my soul and body under your blessed
care and your special protection.

I entrust to you all my hopes and consolations, all my anxieties and sufferings, my entire life, and the final hours of my life.

Through your most holy intercession, grant that all of my works may be directed and carried out according to your will and the will of your divine Son. Amen.

Saint Louis de Montfort

We Fly to Your Protection

We fly to your protection,
O holy Mother of God;
Despise not our petitions in our necessities,
but deliver us always from all dangers,
O glorious and blessed Virgin. Amen.

*Oldest known prayer to the Virgin,
found in a Greek papyrus ca. 300*

To Our Lady of Lourdes

O Immaculate Virgin, Mother of Mercy, Health of the Sick, Refuge of Sinners, Comforter of the Afflicted, no one who ever sought your help was left unaided.

You appeared in the Grotto of Lourdes and made it a sanctuary where you continue to dispense your favors to those who suffer from spiritual and corporal infirmities.

I come before you fully confident in your maternal intercession and ask that you hear my prayer and intercede for me. (*Mention your request*).

Grant me also the grace to imitate your virtues and persevere in leading a life of integrity and holiness.

Our Lady of Lourdes, pray for me and for all my loved ones. Amen.

To Our Lady of the Miraculous Medal

Mary Immaculate, you have given yourself to us as Our Lady of the Miraculous Medal. You have asked us to pray with confidence, and we will receive great graces. We know your compassion because you saw your Son suffer and die for us. In your union with his suffering, you became the mother of us all.

Mary, my mother, teach me to understand my suffering as you do and to endure it in union with the suffering of Jesus. In your motherly love, calm my fears and increase my trust in God's loving care.

According to God's plan, obtain for me the healing I need. Intercede with your Son that I may have the strength I need to work for God's glory and the salvation of the world. Amen.

Mary, health of the sick, pray for us.

To Mary, Undoer of Knots

Virgin Mary, Mother of fair love, Mother who never refuses to come to the aid of a child in need, Mother whose hands never cease to serve your beloved children because they are moved by the divine love and immense mercy that exists in your heart, cast your compassionate eyes upon me and see the snarl of knots that exist in my life.

You know very well how desperate I am, you know my pain and how I am bound by these knots. Mary, Mother to whom God entrusted the undoing of the knots in the lives of his children, I entrust into your hands the ribbon of my life. No one, not even the evil one himself, can take it away from your precious care. In your hands there is no knot that cannot be undone.

Powerful Mother, by your grace and intercessory power with your Son and my Redeemer, Jesus, take into your hands today this knot (*mention your need or intention*). I beg you to undo it for the glory of God, once and for all. You are my hope.

O my Lady, you are the only consolation God gives me, the fortification of my feeble strength, the enrichment of my destitution and, with Christ, the freedom from my chains.

Hear my plea.

Keep me, guide me, protect me, O safe refuge!

Mary, Undoer of Knots, pray for me.

The Holy Rosary

After the Holy Sacrifice of the Mass, the most powerful prayer of the Church is the Rosary. Carrying a rosary with you is like carrying the Gospel with you—or as someone once said, it's like having the Gospel on a string. Praying the Rosary, said Father Peyton, is to contemplate the life of Jesus through Mary's eyes.

Praying the Rosary keeps us close to Mary and her Son Jesus. As we pray over and over the comforting words of the Hail Mary, we are reminded that we have a heavenly Mother who loves us and intercedes for us. No matter what challenges we may face in life, Mary is always there to help us. We can go to her with confidence, knowing she will not let us down. Pray the Rosary daily. Keep a blessed rosary with you, day and night. Reflect on the mysteries as you pray.

Begin the Rosary by making the Sign of the Cross (p. 117); then, while holding the crucifix, pray the Apostles' Creed (p. 118). On the beads following the crucifix pray one Our Father (p.

117), three Hail Marys (p. 117), and a Glory Be (p. 118). Next, read the mystery and pray one Our Father, ten Hail Marys, and a Glory Be. It is recommended to then pray the Fatima Prayer (p. 80). This completes one decade. All the other decades are prayed in the same manner, while pondering the mystery for each decade. Pray the Hail, Holy Queen (p. 80) at the end.

1. Make the Sign of the Cross and pray the Apostles' Creed.
2. Pray the Our Father.
3. Pray 3 Hail Marys.
4. Pray the Glory, name the first Mystery, and pray the Our Father.
5. Pray 10 Hail Marys.
6. Pray the Glory, name the second Mystery, and pray the Our Father.
7. Repeat steps 5 and 6 with each Mystery until you reach the end.
8. Pray the Glory and the Hail, Holy Queen.

Joyful Mysteries

1. The Annunciation of the Angel to Mary
   (Lk 1:26–38)

2. Mary Visits Her Cousin Elizabeth
   (Lk 1:39–40)

3. The Birth of Jesus at Bethlehem
   (Lk 2:1–14)

4. The Presentation of Jesus in the Temple
   (Lk 2:22–34)

5. The Finding of Jesus in the Temple
   (Lk 2:42–48)

Luminous Mysteries

1. John Baptizes Jesus in the Jordan
   (Mt 3:13–17)

2. Christ Reveals His Glory at the
   Wedding at Cana (Jn 2:1–11)

3. Jesus Proclaims the Kingdom of God and
   Calls Us to Conversion
   (Mk 1:14–15)

4. The Transfiguration of Jesus
   (Mk 9:2–8)

5. Jesus Institutes the Eucharist
   (Mk 14:22–25)

Sorrowful Mysteries

1. Jesus Prays in the Garden of Gethsemane
   (Mk 14:32–42)

2. Jesus Is Scourged
   (Mk 15:15)

3. Jesus Is Crowned with Thorns
   (Mt 27:27–31)

4. Jesus Carries the Cross to Calvary
   (Lk 23:26–32)

5. Jesus Is Crucified
   (Lk 23:33–49; Jn 19:25–27)

Glorious Mysteries

1. Jesus Rises from the Dead
   (Mt 28:1–6)

2. Jesus Ascends into Heaven
   (Acts 1:9–11)

3. The Holy Spirit Descends on Mary and the
   Apostles (Acts 2:1–4)

4. Mary Is Assumed into Heaven
   (Jn 14:3)

5. Mary Is Crowned Queen of Heaven and
   Earth (Rev 12:1)

Fatima Prayer

O my Jesus, forgive us our sins. Save us from the fires of hell. Lead all souls to heaven, especially those who have most need of your mercy.

Hail, Holy Queen

Hail, holy Queen, Mother of mercy, our life, our sweetness, and our hope! To you do we cry, poor banished children of Eve. To you do we send up our sighs, mourning, and weeping in this valley of tears. Turn then, most gracious advocate, your eyes of mercy toward us; and after this our exile, show unto us the blessed fruit of your womb, Jesus. O clement, O loving, O sweet Virgin Mary.

V. Pray for us, O Holy Mother of God.

R. That we may be made worthy of the promises of Christ.

O God, whose only-begotten Son, by His life, death, and resurrection, has purchased for us the rewards of eternal life, grant, we beseech Thee, that meditating on the mysteries of the most holy Rosary of the Blessed Virgin Mary, we may imitate what they contain, and obtain what they promise, through the same Christ our Lord. Amen.

Prayers to the Angels
and the Saints

Prayer to Saint Raphael for Healing

Almighty and eternal God, healer of those who trust in you, through the intercession of Saint Raphael, Archangel, hear my prayer for (*name*). In your tender mercy, restore her/him to spiritual and/or bodily health that she/he may give you thanks, praise your name, and proclaim your wondrous love to all. I ask this through Christ your Son, our Lord. Amen.

Saint Raphael, health of the sick, pray for us!

Prayer to Saint Raphael in Time of Need

Blessed Saint Raphael, Archangel, I ask your help in my time of need. Through the power of God, you restored sight to Tobit and gave guidance to young Tobiah. Intercede for me now that my soul may be healed and my body protected from all ills, so that through the help of divine grace I may one day dwell in the eternal glory of God in heaven. Amen.

Memorare to Saint Joseph

Remember, O chaste Spouse of the Virgin Mary, that never has it been known that anyone who asked for your help or sought your intercession was left unaided. Inspired by this confidence, I commend myself to you and beg your protection. Despise not my petition, dear foster father of our Redeemer, but hear and answer my prayer. Amen.

Prayer of Intercession to Saint Jude

Most Holy Apostle, Saint Jude, patron saint of impossible causes, I place myself in your care. With fervent trust and confidence, I seek your heavenly intercession. Pray for me in my times of need. Help me realize each day that I am not alone when facing sickness, disease, suffering, or sorrow.

Assist me now, dear Saint Jude, in petitioning Almighty God for strength when I am in distress, courage to overcome my anxieties, and the gift of a complete healing of mind and body. Ask our loving Lord to deepen my faith and steadfast conviction in his healing power and to bless me with the graces necessary to accept whatever may lie ahead for me and for my loved ones.

Thank you, O holy Saint Jude, for the promise of hope you offer to all who believe. Inspire me always to offer this gift of hope to others. Amen.

Prayer to Saint Dymphna

Dearest Saint Dymphna, great wonder-worker in every affliction of mind and body, I humbly implore your powerful intercession with Jesus through Mary, the Health of the Sick and Comforter of the Afflicted. May both Mary and you present my request to Jesus, the Divine Physician.

You are filled with love and compassion for the many who invoke your name. Show the same love and compassion toward me as I turn to you now. The many miracles and cures which have been wrought through your intercession give me great confidence that you will help me in my present illness (*mention it*).

Saint Dymphna, through your glorious martyrdom for the love of Christ, help me to be loyal to my faith and my God for as long as I live. Patroness of those who suffer distress of mind and nervous afflictions, pray to Jesus and Mary for me and obtain my request.

Pray one Our Father, one Hail Mary, and one Glory Be.

Saint Dymphna, virgin and martyr, pray for us.

Novena Prayer to Saint Peregrine

O glorious wonder-worker, Saint Peregrine, you answered the divine call with a ready spirit. You left all the comforts of a life of ease and all the empty honors of the world to dedicate yourself to God in the order of his most holy Mother. You labored zealously and tirelessly for the salvation of people and in union with Jesus crucified, you endured the most painful sufferings with such patience that you were healed miraculously of an incurable cancer. With a touch of the divine hand your leg wound disappeared.

Obtain for me the grace to answer every call of God and to fulfill his will in all the events of life. Enkindle in my heart a consuming zeal for the salvation of all people. Deliver me from the infirmities that afflict my body (*state your intention here*).

Obtain for me perfect resignation in my sufferings. Imitating your virtues and tenderly loving our crucified Lord and his sorrowful Mother, may I be enabled to merit eternal glory in heaven. Amen.

Prayer to Saint Rita for a Special Intention

Holy patroness of those in need, you suffered through a long illness and showed your love for Jesus Crucified through patient forbearance. Teach me how to pray so that I may join my sufferings with those of Jesus.

Filled with confidence in your intercession, I ask that you come to the aid of (*name*) in his/her time of need. Trusting that all things are possible to God, I place my petition in your hands, that this healing may give glory to God and proclaim his love to the ends of the earth. Amen.

Litany for the Sick and the Afflicted in Body and Spirit

Lord, *have mercy.*

Christ, *have mercy.*

Lord, *have mercy.*

Christ, *hear us.*

Christ, *graciously hear us.*

   Response: Have mercy on us.

God, the Father of Heaven, *R.*

God the Son, Redeemer of the World, *R.*

God the Holy Spirit, *R.*

Holy Trinity, One God, *R.*

Jesus, Divine Redeemer, *R.*

Jesus, author of life, *R.*

Jesus, Good Shepherd, *R.*

Jesus, Divine Physician, *R.*

Jesus, healer of all our ills, *R.*

Jesus, comforter in every affliction, *R.*

Jesus, who suffered for our offenses, *R.*

Jesus, crucified for our salvation, *R.*

Jesus, resurrected in glory, *R.*

   Response: Pray for us.

Holy Mary, *R.*

Holy Mother of God, *R.*

Mother of mercy, *R.*

Mother of divine grace, *R.*

Mother of perpetual help, *R.*

Mother of hope, *R.*

Mother, whose heart was pierced by a sword, *R.*

Mother of a lost child, *R.*

Mother, who endures our sorrows and shares
   our joys, *R.*

Woman, who lived as an immigrant in Egypt, *R.*

Woman, widowed by a husband's death, *R.*

Woman, who stood at the cross of your
   crucified Son, *R.*

Our Lady of Prompt Succor, *R.*

Health of the sick, Comforter of the afflicted, *R.*

Help of Christians, *R.*

Saint Jude and Saint Rita, patrons of desperate cases, *R.*

Saints Mary Magdalene, Anthony Abbot, Benedict and John Vianney, intercessors for those tormented by evil spirits, *R.*

Saints Dymphna and Benedict Joseph Labre, helpers of all afflicted with mental anguish or illness, *R.*

Saint Pio of Pietrelcina, guardian of those suffering from stress and depression, *R.*

Saint Vitus and Saint Giles, protectors of those who suffer from epilepsy, *R.*

Saint Thorlak, advocate for the autistic, *R.*

Saints Peregrine, Agatha, and Blessed Chiara Badano, patrons of cancer patients, *R.*

Saint John of God, intercessor for those with heart problems and heart disease, *R.*

Saint Andrew of Avellino, patron saint of stroke victims, *R.*

Saint John Paul II, saint of those with Parkinson's disease, *R.*

Saints Wolfgang, Julie Billiart and Blessed Anne Catherine Emmerich, guardians of those suffering from paralysis, *R.*

Saint Gemma Galgani, helper for all suffering from spinal diseases and injuries, *R.*

Saint Margaret Mary Alacoque and Blessed Pier Giorgio Frassati, intercessors of polio sufferers, *R.*

Saints Thérèse of Lisieux and Gabriel Possenti, patrons of tuberculosis patients, *R.*

Saint Elizabeth of the Trinity, guardian of those suffering from Addison's disease, *R.*

Saint Bernadette Soubirous, protector of all afflicted with respiratory diseases, *R.*

Saints Raphael, Lucy, Clare, and Blessed Margaret of Costello, intercessors for all who suffer from blindness and diseases of the eye, *R.*

Saint Francis de Sales, patron saint of those suffering from deafness and ear ailments, *R.*

Saint Blaise, protector against all afflictions of the throat, *R.*

Saint Apollonia, helper of those who suffer from toothaches and diseases of the mouth, *R.*

Saints Peter Damien, Teresa of Ávila and Rita of Cascia, intercessors for those afflicted by migraines and severe headaches, *R.*

Saint Margaret of Antioch and Saint Benedict, guardians against kidney disease, *R.*

Saints Felix and Gertrude, protectors of those afflicted with fever, *R.*

Saint Josemaría Escrivá, patron of diabetes sufferers, *R.*

Saint Erasmus, helper for all with intestinal problems, liver disease, or appendicitis, *R.*

Saint Germaine and Blessed Margaret of Costello, advocates of all with physical disabilities, *R.*

Saint Anthony of Padua, guardian of amputees, *R.*

Saints James the Apostle and Alphonsus de Liguori, patrons of all arthritis sufferers, *R.*

Saints Lidwina and Juliana, intercessors for all suffering from chronic illness and pain, *R.*

Saints André Bessette and Charbel Makhlouf, healers of the sick, *R.*

Saint Catherine of Alexandria, protector against sudden death, *R.*

Saint Nicholas of Tolentino and Saint Teresa of Calcutta, assistants of the dying, *R.*

Saint Joseph, patron of the dying, *R.*

Saints Joachim and Anne, intercessors of couples desiring children, *R.*

Saint Gerard Majella, patron of expectant mothers and those trying to conceive, *R.*

Saints Paul VI and Gianna Beretta Molla, guardians of the unborn and helpers in difficult pregnancies, *R.*

Saints Thomas More and Louis Martin, patrons of widowers, *R.*

Saints Monica, Elizabeth Ann Seton, and Marguerite d'Youville, helpers of widows, *R.*

Saint Augustine, patron of prodigal children,

Saint Germaine Cousin and Blessed Margaret of Costello, protectors of unwanted, abused, or abandoned children, *R.*

Saint Teresa of Calcutta, guardian of outcasts,

Saint Josephine Bakhita, protector of victims of human trafficking, *R.*

Saints Augustine and Margaret of Cortona, intercessors against sexual temptation, *R.*

Saint Maria Goretti and Blessed Alexandrina di Costa, helpers of survivors of sexual assault and intercessors for those addicted to pornography, *R.*

Saints Monica, Rita and Blessed Anna Maria Taigi, protectors of wives who suffer abuse, *R.*

Saints Rita and Marguerite d'Youville, intercessors for difficult marriages, *R.*

Saint Monica and Saint Matthias, patrons of alcoholics, *R.*

Saint Maximilian Kolbe, guardian against drug abuse and advocate of prisoners, *R.*

Saint Bernadino, helper of those addicted to gambling, *R.*

Saint Jude, helper of all struggling with addiction, *R.*

Saint Benedict, protector against poisoning, *R.*

Saints Nicholas of Myra and Gerard Majella, advocates for the falsely accused, *R.*

Saints Martin de Porres and Josephine Bakhita, advocates for racial justice, *R.*

Saint Frances Cabrini, advocate for the immigrant, *R.*

Saint Cajetan, patron of the unemployed seeking work, *R.*

Saints Benedict Joseph Labre and Elizabeth of Hungary, protectors of the homeless, *R.*

Saint Kateri Tekawitha, intercessor for those afflicted with smallpox, *R.*

Saints Damien de Veuster and Marianne Cope, patrons of those suffering from Hansen's disease and advocates of those with AIDS, *R.*

Saint Rosalie, helper in epidemics, *R.*

Saint Casimir, protector against widespread illness, *R.*

Saint Florian, protector against fire and floods, *R.*

Saint Guy, protector against lightning, *R.*

Saint Emygidius, protector against earthquakes, *R.*

Saints Medard and Saint Barbara, protectors from hurricanes and tornadoes, *R.*

You fourteen holy helpers, guardians against pandemics and against natural disasters, *R.*

Saint John the Evangelist, patron of caregivers, *R.*

Saint Luke and Saint Giuseppe Moscati, and all patrons of physicians, *R.*

Saints Luke, Barbara, Cosmas, and Damian, patrons of surgeons, *R.*

Saints Raphael, Agatha, Catherine of Siena, and all patrons of nurses, *R.*

Saint Michael, patron of paramedics and first responders, *R.*

Saint Camillus de Lellis, patron of health care and hospice workers, *R.*

Saints Raphael, Mary Magdalene, Cosmas, and Damian, and all patrons of pharmacists, *R.*

Saint Michael and Blessed Cecilia Schelingová, patrons of radiologists, *R.*

Saint Lucy, patron of ophthalmologists and opticians, *R.*

Saint Apollonia, patron of dentists, *R*.

Saints Raymund Nonnatus, Brigid of Ireland, Margaret of Cortona, patrons of midwives and obstetricians, *R*.

Saints Aloysius Gonzaga, Damien de Veuster, and Marianne Cope, patrons of AIDS caregivers, *R*.

Saints Dymphna and Christina, patrons of mental health professionals and caregivers, *R*.

Saint John Regis, patron of medical social workers, *R*.

Saint Martha, patron of dieticians, *R*.

All you saints of the medical profession, *R*.

Prayers for a Good Death
and for the Dying

Prayer to Mary for a Good Death

O Mary, conceived without sin, pray for us who have recourse to you. Refuge of sinners, Mother of the dying, be with us at the hour of our death. Intercede for us that we may have sincere sorrow and the remission of our sins. Pray that we might have the grace to receive the last sacraments of Anointing, Penance, and Viaticum worthily so as to stand confidently before the throne of Jesus Christ, our just and merciful Redeemer. Amen.

Prayer to Saint Joseph for a Happy Death

Saint Joseph, protector of the dying, I ask you to intercede for all the dying, and I invoke your assistance in the hour of my own death. You merited a happy passing by a holy life, and in your last hours you had the great consolation of being assisted by Jesus and Mary. Deliver me from sudden death; obtain for me the grace to imitate you in life, to detach my heart from everything worldly, and daily to gather treasures for the moment of my death. Obtain for me the grace to receive the sacrament of the sick well, and with Mary, fill my heart with sentiments of faith, hope, love, and sorrow for sins, so that I may breathe forth my soul in peace. Amen.

Blessed James Alberione

Invocations for a Holy Death

Jesus, Mary, and Joseph, I give you my heart and my soul.

Jesus, Mary, and Joseph, assist me in the hour of my death.

Jesus, Mary, and Joseph, may I breathe forth my soul in peace with you.

Prayer for Perseverance

Oh, my Lord and Savior, support me in that hour in the strong arms of your sacraments, and by the fresh fragrance of your consolations. Let the absolving words be said over me, and the holy oil sign and seal me, and your own Body be my food, and your Blood my sprinkling; and let my sweet Mother, Mary, breathe on me, and my angel whisper peace to me, and my glorious Saints (*name them*) smile upon me; that in them all, and through them all, I may receive the gift of perseverance, and die, as I desire to live, in your faith, in your Church, in your service, and in your love. Amen.

Saint John Henry Newman

For Those at the Point of Death

O Saint Joseph, protector of those in their last moments of life, take pity on those who are suffering their final battle. Take pity on my soul, too, when the hour of death shall come upon me. Do not abandon me but show that you are my good father and grant me your assistance. In your kindness intercede for me that my divine Savior may receive me with mercy into that dwelling where the elect enjoy life that shall never end! Amen.

Invocations for the Dying

Eternal Father, by your love for Saint Joseph whom you chose from among all men to represent your divine fatherhood here on earth, have mercy on us and on all those who will die this day.

Our Father, Hail Mary, Glory Be.

Eternal Son, by your love for Saint Joseph who was your faithful guardian on earth, have mercy on us and on all those who will die this day.

Our Father, Hail Mary, Glory Be.

Eternal Spirit, by your love for Saint Joseph who so carefully watched over Mary, your beloved spouse, have mercy on us and on all those who will die this day.

Our Father, Hail Mary, Glory Be.

Sacrament of Anointing of the Sick

We should call a priest when someone becomes dangerously ill due to sickness, accident, or old age, so that he or she may receive grace and consolation from the sacrament of Anointing of the Sick. Christ's minister should be called to visit the sick in any serious illness even when death does not seem near.

The elderly who are in a weakened condition are also encouraged by the Church to receive the Anointing of the Sick, even though no dangerous illness is present. The sacrament should be repeated each time there is a worsening of the person's condition, as well as before any serious operation. Penance and Eucharist are usually received along with the Anointing of the Sick.

This sacrament can be received at home or in a hospital. At home, prepare a table near the sick person. Cover the table with a clean white cloth. On the table you may place, if possible, a crucifix, two candles and some holy water.

Those who are in danger of death should be told of their condition so that they may prepare themselves to receive Christ in the sacraments. It is recommended to call a priest before a person loses consciousness. In case of sudden or unexpected death, always call a priest, because absolution and the anointing can be given conditionally for some time after apparent death.

The priest administers the sacrament of Anointing of the Sick by anointing the forehead and hands of the person with blessed oil, while praying the words of the sacrament.

Through this sacrament, the Holy Spirit

— strengthens the sick person to deal with the difficulties of illness;

— forgives sins;

— sometimes gives physical healing;

— unites the sick person with Christ's passion, so that suffering takes on new meaning;

— for those who are approaching death, prepares them for this final journey.

It is strongly recommended to pray the Divine Mercy Chaplet (p. 46) with anyone who is at the point of death. The following prayers can also be used.

To Saint Joseph for the Dying

Saint Joseph, foster father of our Lord Jesus Christ, and true spouse of the Virgin Mary, pray for us and for the dying of this day.

For a Dying Person

Remember not, O Lord, we implore you, the sins of your servant, but in your great mercy be mindful of him/her in this moment of passing from mortal life to eternal life. Open paradise and let the angels rejoice as they welcome him/her. Into your kingdom, O Lord, receive your servant.

O Mother of God and our Mother, loving consoler of the afflicted, commend to your Son Jesus the soul of (*name*). Through your maternal intercession, may he/she not fear the terrors of death, but feel instead your reassuring presence. Obtain for him/her a joyful entry into heaven.

Saint Joseph, patron of the dying, who at your death was assisted by Jesus and Mary, come to the aid of (*name*). Obtain for him/her deliverance from eternal death and attainment to heavenly joys. Amen.

Litany for the Dying

Lord, *have mercy on us.*

Christ, *have mercy on us.*

Lord, *have mercy on us.*

   Response: Pray for him/her.

Holy Mary, *R.*

All you holy angels and archangels, *R.*

Holy Abel, *R.*

All you choirs of the just, *R.*

Holy Abraham, *R.*

Saint John the Baptist, *R.*

Saint Joseph, *R.*

All you patriarchs and prophets, *R.*

Saint Peter, *R.*

Saint Paul, *R.*

Saint Andrew, *R.*

Saint John, *R.*

All you holy apostles and evangelists, *R.*

All you holy disciples of the Lord, *R.*

All you holy innocents, *R.*

Saint Stephen, *R.*

Saint Lawrence, *R.*

All you holy martyrs, *R.*

Saint Sylvester, *R.*

Saint Gregory, *R.*

Saint Augustine, *R.*

All you holy bishops and confessors, *R.*

Saint Benedict, *R.*

Saint Dominic, *R.*

Saint Francis, *R.*

All you holy monks and hermits, *R.*

Saint Mary Magdalene, *R.*

Saint Lucy, *R.*

All you holy virgins and widows, *R.*

All you saints of God, *intercede for him/her.*

Be merciful, *spare him/her, O Lord.*

Response: Deliver him/her, O Lord.

Be merciful, *R.*

From sudden death, *R.*

From violent death, *R.*

From the pains of hell, *R.*

From the power of the devil, *R.*

From all evil, *R.*

By your nativity, *R.*

By your cross and passion, *R.*

By your death and burial, *R.*

By your glorious resurrection, *R.*

By your admirable ascension, *R.*

By the grace of the Holy Spirit, the Comforter, *R.*

In the day of judgment, *we beseech you, hear us.*

That you spare him, *we beseech you, hear us.*

Lord, *have mercy on us.*

Christ, *have mercy on us.*

Lord, *have mercy on us.*

Then when the moment of death seems near, the Priest (or any person) recites the following:

Prayer of Commendation

Go forth, Christian soul, from this world
in the name of God, the almighty Father,
who created you,
in the name of Jesus Christ, Son of the
    living God,
who suffered for you,
in the name of the Holy Spirit,
who was poured out upon you,
go forth, faithful Christian.
May you live in peace this day,
may your home be with God in Zion,
with Mary, the virgin Mother of God,
with Joseph, and all the angels and saints.

Basic Prayers

The Sign of the Cross

In the name of the Father, and of the Son, and of the Holy Spirit. Amen.

The Lord's Prayer (Our Father)

Our Father, who art in heaven, hallowed be thy name; thy kingdom come; thy will be done on earth as it is in heaven. Give us this day our daily bread, and forgive us our trespasses, as we forgive those who trespass against us, and lead us not into temptation, but deliver us from evil. Amen.

Hail Mary

Hail Mary, full of grace, the Lord is with thee. Blessed are thou among women, and blessed is the fruit of thy womb, Jesus. Holy Mary, Mother of God, pray for us sinners, now and at the hour of our death. Amen.

Glory Be

Glory be to the Father and to the Son and to the Holy Spirit. As it was in the beginning, is now, and ever shall be, world without end. Amen.

The Apostles' Creed

I believe in God, the Father almighty,
Creator of heaven and earth,
and in Jesus Christ, his only Son, our Lord,
who was conceived by the Holy Spirit,
born of the Virgin Mary, suffered under
    Pontius Pilate,
was crucified, died, and was buried;
he descended into hell; on the third day
    he rose again from the dead;
he ascended into heaven, and is seated at the
    right hand of God, the Father almighty;
from there he will come to judge the living
    and the dead.
I believe in the Holy Spirit, the holy catholic
    Church,

the communion of saints, the forgiveness
of sins,
the resurrection of the body, and life
everlasting. Amen.

.

Notes

1. Mt 9:20–22; Mk 5:25–34; Lk 8:43–48.

2. Originally published, untitled, in *Prayers for Surviving Depression*, Kathryn J. Hermes, FSP (Boston: Pauline Books & Media, 2004), 149.

3. Ibid. 157.

4. Gabriele Amorth, SSP, *An Exorcist Tells His Story*, from "Prayer for Inner Healing" (San Francisco: Ignatius Press, 1999), 201.

5. Mary Peter Martin, FSP, *Tender Mercies: Prayers for Healing and Coping* (Boston: Pauline Books & Media, 2007), 35.

6. The Litany of Trust written by Sr. Faustina Maria Pia, SV; Sisters of Life (sistersoflife.org). Originally published on https://sistersoflife.org/wp-content/uploads/2019/07/Mobile-Litany-of-Trust.pdf.

7. Reverend Joe Coleman, *Hope-Filled Prayers* (Boston: Pauline Books & Media, 2000), 79.

8. Ibid., 80.

List of Contributors

All prayers were taken from common sources, with the exception of those credited in the text and the following:

Gabriele Amorth, SSP

Mary Peter Martin, FSP

Faustina Maria Pia, Sister of Life

Reverend Joe Coleman

Brian Moore, SJ

Mary Martha Moss, FSP

Mary Leonora Wilson, FSP

BOOKS & MEDIA

A mission of the Daughters of St. Paul

As apostles of Jesus Christ,
evangelizing today's world:

We are CALLED to holiness
by God's living Word and Eucharist.

We COMMUNICATE the Gospel message
through our lives and through all
available forms of media.

We SERVE the Church
by responding to the hopes and needs
of all people with the Word of God,
in the spirit of St. Paul.

For more information visit us at:
www.pauline.org.

Pauline
BOOKS & MEDIA

The Daughters of St. Paul operate book and media centers at the following addresses. Visit, call, or write the one nearest you today, or find us at www.paulinestore.org.

CALIFORNIA
3908 Sepulveda Blvd, Culver City, CA 90230 — 310-397-8676
3250 Middlefield Road, Menlo Park, CA 94025 — 650-562-7060

FLORIDA
145 S.W. 107th Avenue, Miami, FL 33174 — 305-559-6715

HAWAII
1143 Bishop Street, Honolulu, HI 96813 — 808-521-2731

ILLINOIS
172 North Michigan Avenue, Chicago, IL 60601 — 312-346-4228

LOUISIANA
4403 Veterans Memorial Blvd, Metairie, LA 70006 — 504-887-7631

MASSACHUSETTS
885 Providence Hwy, Dedham, MA 02026 — 781-326-5385

MISSOURI
9804 Watson Road, St. Louis, MO 63126 — 314-965-3512

NEW YORK
115 E. 29th Street, New York City, NY 10016 — 212-754-1110

SOUTH CAROLINA
243 King Street, Charleston, SC 29401 — 843-577-0175

VIRGINIA
1025 King Street, Alexandria, VA 22314 — 703-549-3806

CANADA
3022 Dufferin Street, Toronto, ON M6B 3T5 — 416-781-9131

Special Bulk Prices Available!*

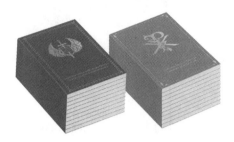

Get multiple copies of *Essential Healing Prayers for Peace and Strength* and *Essential Spiritual Warfare Prayers for Protection and Deliverance* for gifts, parish groups, RCIA candidates and catechumens, friends, and family.

> 20 + for $6 each
> 50 + for $5 each
> 100 + for $4 each

For U.S. bulk orders, online ordering available at https://paulinestore.com/healing-prayers or visit your local Pauline Books & Media book store.

For Canadian bulk orders, online ordering available at https://paulinestore.ca/healing-prayers or visit our Pauline Books & Media book store in Toronto.

*Prices subject to change. Bulk offer for trade and wholesale customers is net.